I am Proud of my Family

Estoy Orgulloso de mi Familia
Iyi Cusiji'ini Shi'in Na Ta'in

In English, Spanish, and Mixteco

George Feldman, David Bacon, and Natalia Gracida Cruz

English and Spanish texts are by George Feldman.

Mixteco and Spanish texts are by Natalia Gracida Cruz.

Poems are by Natalia Gracida Cruz, and translated by Dana Romo and Manuel Barajas.

All photos, except the final photo, are by David Bacon copyright © 2012.

The final photo is by George Feldman.

To our newest citizens. -George Feldman

To the people in our pictures. -David Bacon

To Ariel Benson for her support. -Natalia Gracida Cruz

I am Mixteco, and my family is part of California.

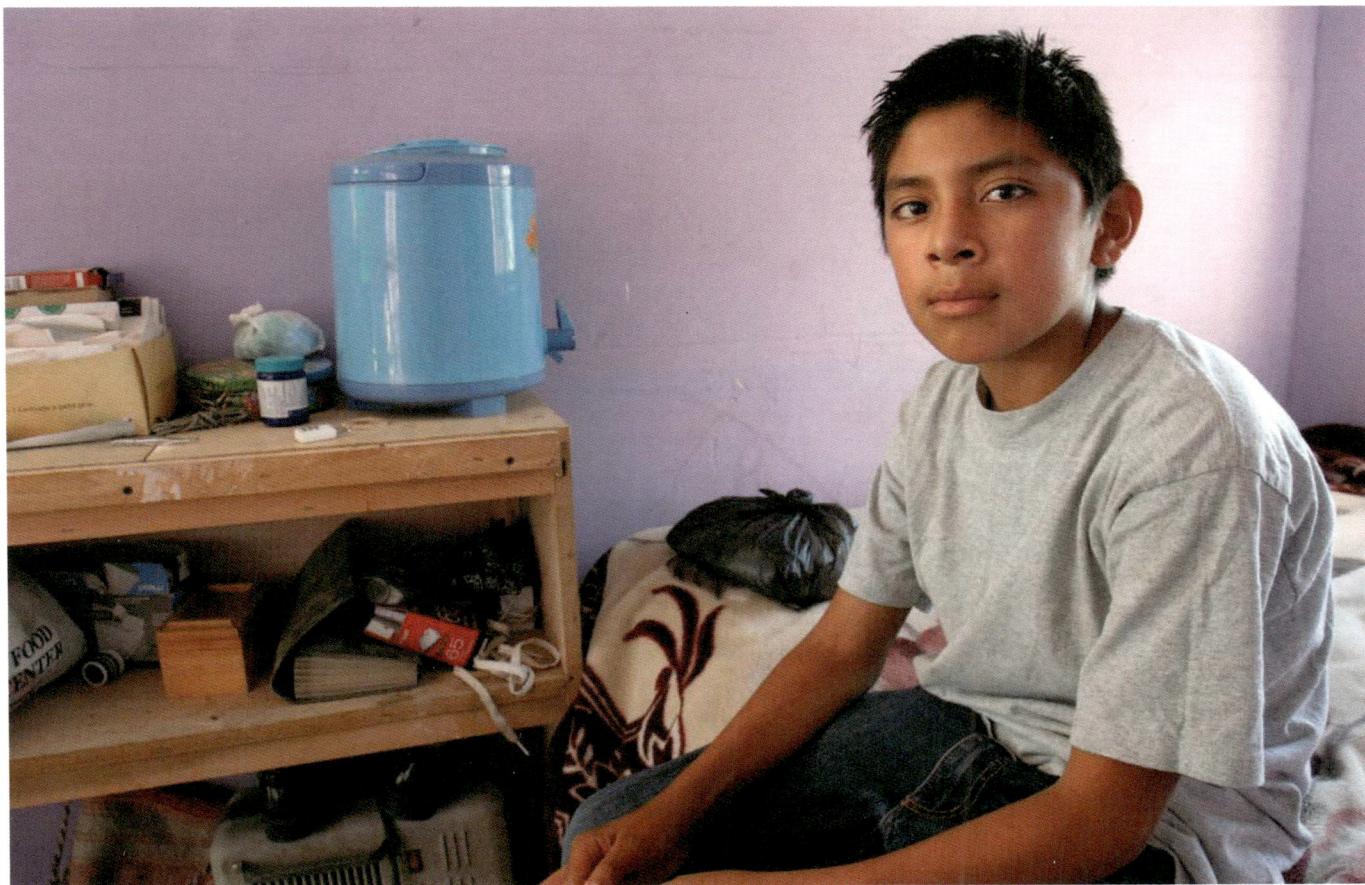

Photo copyright © 2012 by David Bacon

Soy Mixteco y mi familia es parte de California.

Ra, ca'am thuun thavicki sati na ta, in dhena Norte yo,o'.

My uncle prepares the watermelon.

Mi tió prepara la sándia.

Shiti kisha prepara'ra sandia.

My father
packages the
zucchini.

*Mi papá empaca
las calabacitas.*

**Tati kisha empaca,
ra Ykinvali,i.**

My cousin waters
the strawberries.

*Mi primo riega
la fresa.*

Ñani cuachi
cosora fresa.

My aunt harvests
blueberries.

Mi tía cosecha los
arándanos azules.

Shi,shi sán zhiejeña
ri arando zhi,i.

My mother sorts
out the good onions.

*Mi mamá separa las
cebollas buenas.*

Nani saculliyo ña
zhicomi ba,a.

My grandmother grows
the flower garden.

Mi abuela siembra
el jardín de flores.

Nana lani sanzheje
ña ita lle,e,ña.

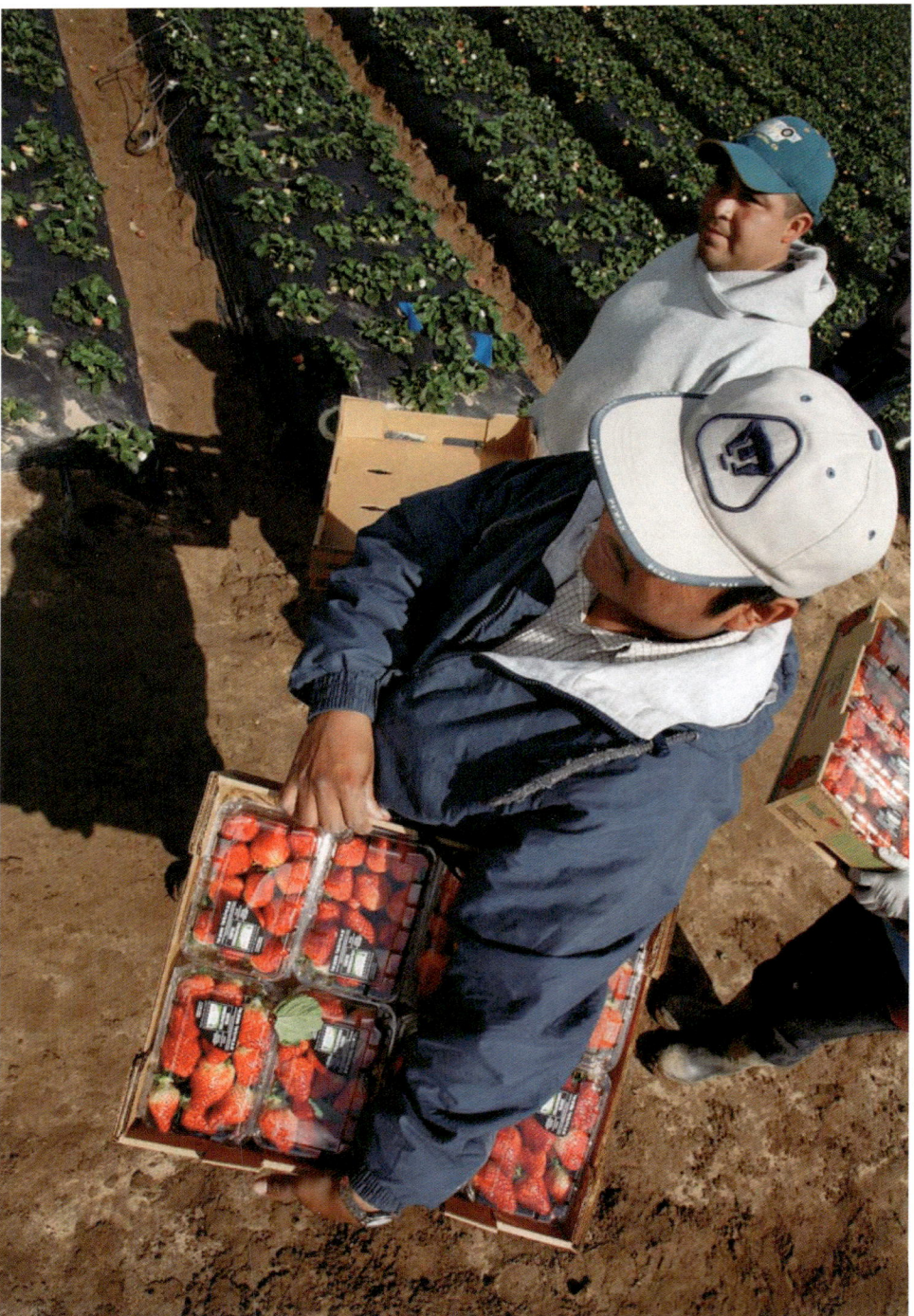

My grandfather delivers the strawberries.

Mi abuelo entrega las fresas.

Tata lani ishicora fresas.

All of California
eats our harvests.

California come
nuestras cosechas.

Na norte yo'o na
shi shi na ña
chi'iee.

Notes on Mixteco languages and spellings

The term Mixteco language is a misnomer; there are actually about 25 related Mixteco languages. They are spoken by about 500,000 indigenous speakers, mostly from Oaxaca, a state in Mexico. According to mixteco.org, about 100,000 Mixtecos will live part of their lives in the US.

From 2010-12 about 25% of George Feldman's first grade students in Watsonville, California were Mixteco.

La Academia de la Lengua Mixteca is currently regularizing written Mixteco languages.

We have used –zh- to make the /j/ like sound.

For more information

You can see more of David Bacon's photos at his website, http://dbacon.igc.org/

An excellent thesis on Mixteco students in US schools by Ana Kovats is at http://sdsu-dspace.calstate.edu/xmlui/bitstream/handle/10211.10/520/Kovats_Ana.pdf?sequence=1

Advocacy and informational groups include

California Rural Legal Assistance, http://www.crla.org/indigenous-farmworker-project

Frente indígena de organizaciones binacionales, http://fiob.org

Instituto Oaxaqueño de Atención al Migrante, http://www.migrantes.oaxaca.gob.mx/

Summer Institute of Language, http://www.sil.org/mexico/mixteca/00i-mixteca.htm

Ventura County Mixteca/Indigina Community Organizing Project,
    http://www.mixteco.org

Las circunstancias

Mamá

Me vine en busca de una vida mejor
creyendo que era fácil, pero no.
Tuve que enfrentarme a cosas muy
difíciles.
Fue cuando me di cuenta
que pisando la tierra Americana
hay dos caminos.

Una de Ellas es para ganar
y otra a la perdición.
Tuve que ser fuerte y luchar
para poder encontrar el camino de la luz.
Y espero poder caminar en ese camino
con mucho cuidado para no perderme.

Gracias por tus consejos mama.
Gracias por el amor que me diste
porque tu amor es incondicional.
Me siento muy orgulloso/a
de tener una madre como tú.

Porque tus palabras y tus cariños
me hicieron fuerte.
Tus sonrisas y tus abrazos
me ayudaron para luchar.
Aunque estoy lejos de ti mamá,
sigo siendo la misma.

Aunque han pasado muchos años,
no me he olvidado de ti mamá.
He aprendido hablar español.
Ahora, estoy aprendiendo inglés,
pero nunca dejaré de hablar mi idioma
natal.

No te preocupes mamá. Te prometo
que el Mixteco nunca lo dejaré de hablar.
Siempre podrás y podré comunicarme
con ustedes mamá, papá y con mis
abuelitos, en nuestro idioma natal.

Natalia Gracida Cruz, 4/8/11

The Circumstances

Mother

I came in search of a better life
thinking that it would be easy, but no.
I had to confront some very difficult things.
This is when I discovered
that stepping on American soil
has two paths.

One of them is to win
and the other, great loss.
I had to be strong and fight
to be able to find the enlightened path.
And I hope to be able to walk this path with
caution, so that I don't get lost.

Thank you mother for your wise words.
Thank you for the love you gave me,
because your love is unconditional.
I feel very proud
to have a mother like you.

Because your words and your affection
made me strong.
Your hugs and smiles
helped me to fight.
Even though I am far away from you, mother
I am still the same person.

Even though many years have passed
I haven't forgotten you mother.
I have learned to speak Spanish.
Now, I am learning English,
but I will never stop speaking my native language.

Do not worry mother. I promise
I will never stop speaking the Mixteco language.
You will always and I will always be able to communicate
with you mother, father, and with my
grandparents in our native language.

Natalia Gracida Cruz , Translated by Dana Romo

El Sueño Americano y el reto

Soy de Oaxaca, hablo Mixteco.
Ahora estoy en la tierra Americana.
Donde hablan inglés y español.
Para mí no es fácil.
Porque yo no hablo inglés ni español.

Yo solamente hablo Mixteco.
Cuando mis compañeros me hablan.
No quiero contestarles porque no sé como
contestarles
Por eso se burlan de mí, me humillan.
A veces me siento sin fuerzas. No puedo hacer
nada.

Y me pongo a pensar muchas cosas.
Sí hay algo en mi físico que si puedo cambiar.
Pero otras cosas no.
Puedo cambiar el color de mi cabello.
Pero el color de mi piel no lo puedo cambiar.

Ni mi estatura tampoco porque soy bajita
Por eso la gente desde lejos me distingue.
Que soy de Oaxaca.
Al fin, llegue a la conclusión que soy de Oaxaca
Y eso nadie lo puede cambiar.

Hablo Mixteco y no lo dejaré de hablar.
Soy bajito, así seré siempre.
Mi piel es morena y así será siempre.
Al fin, me acepto como soy.
Me siento orgullosa de ser quien soy.

¡¡Pero eso sí!!

Hay dos metas que quiero alcanzar.
Sí caminé milla y milla para llegar aquí
A la tierra Americana
Y ahora tengo que caminar milla y millas.
Para alcanzar mi meta.

Aprenderé el inglés y el español.
Estoy segura que así será.
Mi sueño se cumplirá.
Al fin, me siento orgullosa de ser quien soy.
Hablaré tres idiomas.

Mixteco, español e inglés.

Llegaré donde tengo que llegar.

Natalia Gracida Cruz, 4/7/11

The Dream and the Challenge

I am from Oaxaca; I speak Mixteco.
Now I am on American land
Where English and Spanish are spoken.
For me this is not easy
Because I do not speak English or Spanish.

I only speak Mixteco.
When my peers speak to me
I don't want to respond because I don't know how to respond.
Because of this they make fun of me, they humiliate me.
Sometimes, I feel weak. I can't do anything.

I begin to wonder about many things.
Yes, there are some physical features I can change,
But there are others I can't.
I can change the color of my hair,
But my skin color cannot be changed.

Not even my height because I am short.
That is how people from afar can tell
I am from Oaxaca.
Finally, I arrived at the conclusion that I am from Oaxaca
And this no one can change.

I speak Mixteco and I will not stop.
I am short, as I will be always.
My skin is brown as it will be always.
In the end, I accept myself the way I am.
I am proud to be who I am.

But one thing's for sure!

There are two goals I want to achieve.
Yes, I walked miles and miles to get here,
To this land of America.
And now I have to walk miles and miles
To reach my goal.

I will learn English and Spanish.
I am sure of it.
My dream will come true.
Finally, I feel proud to be who I am.
I will speak three languages.

Mixteco, Spanish and English.

I will get where I need to be.

Natalia Gracida Cruz, 4/7/11
Translated by Manuel Barajas

15984364R00013

Made in the USA
Charleston, SC
29 November 2012